I0411374

HASAN YAHYA

Arabs

&

Columbus

@ Yahya Family Publidhing House

Hadi Yahya 2013

Jerusalem & Volcano Printers

ضمن مشروع إحياء التراث العربي في المهاجر

بدعم من الموسوعة العربية الأمريكية ومعهد التراث العربي ومطابع القدس والبركان

– الولايات المتحدة

Hasan Yahya, Arabs & Columbus

ISBN-13: 978-1482596489
ISBN-10: 1482596482

Manufactured in the United State of America

To

Arab Thought Renaissance

Introduction

No doubt, the Arabs have a sparkling influence on world thoughts. Arab sciences were on top of world civilization in the age of two great Arab dynasties: the Umayyad and the Abbasid as a continuation product of Islamic thoughts started in the time of Muhammad and the Guided Caliphs.

Theology was mixed with new ethical and spiritual culture drastically different from old ethics of Bedouins before Islam.

In my recent book : Great Arab and Muslim Thinkers, I stated the history and achievement of 27 scientists in various aspects of Knowledge. Not on theology alone, but in almost all sciences known in time of these scholars. Such knowledge contributes to world ethics and culture. For example, in natural sciences such as, Mathematics, Geometry, and Calculus, Chemistry and Physics, Astrology and Astronomy, Medicine and geography.

And in Humanities such as History, geography, and social sciences (sociology, psychology,

Anthropology, politics, and communication and several other fields) (1)

There comes Columbus, in the same year when Arabs left Spain, Isabella and Fernando granted their permission for Columbus to start his mysterious journey to discover the new world.

In this book, several writers, Orientalists and native recently followed studying and searching the history of Columbus; they found documented reports show the Arab connection as a genuine contributor factor in the success of Columbus trip to discover the new land.

In this book, we cover how Columbus owes Arabs in his maps used by him and his crew members to discover the New World-America.

Hasan Yahya, Ph.ds

Former Professor of Comparative Sociology

Michigan – USA

February 2013

Columbus Owes Arabs

His Maps to Discover The New World-America.

1

Some historians claim that if Arabs were still in control of Spain when Columbus began his trip for discovery of the new world, America would be a Muslim Country. Unfortunately, Arabs left Spain in the same year 1492 A.D. This saying has its roots in history. Arabic had been the scientific language of most of humankind from the eighth to the 12th century. It is probably for this reason that Columbus, in his own words, considered Arabic to be "the mother of all languages," and why, on his first voyage to the New World, he took with him Luis de Torres, an Arabic-speaking Spaniard, as his interpreter.

Columbus fully expected to land in India, where he knew that the Arabs had preceded him. He also knew that, for the past five centuries, Arabs had explored, and written of, the far reaches of the known world. They had been around the perimeter of Africa and sailed as far as India. They had ventured overland beyond Constantinople, past Asia Minor, across Egypt and Syria--then the western marches of the unknown Orient--and into the heart of the

Asian continent. They had mapped the terrain, traced the course of rivers, timed the monsoons, scaled mountains, charted shoals and reached China, and, as a result, had spread Islam and the Arabic language in all these regions.(2)

It was on the 33rd day of his voyage, October 12, 1492, that Columbus made his landfall. At that point, he probably stood on the shores of a Bahamian island named Guanahani--which he immediately renamed San Salvador and claimed for "their sovereign majesties, the king and queen of Spain." Probably the first of his surprises that day was his discovery that the "Indians," as he called the islanders he greeted, did not speak Arabic. Still, he remained undaunted and wrote in his log for Friday, October 12, that he was certain he had only to sail on through these outer islands of India to reach the riches of Cipangu (Japan) and China, a journey of only a further 1000 miles. Here, he was convinced, he would greet the Great Khan, an emperor of vast wealth who spoke Arabic and ruled over lands of gold, silver and gems, silks, spices and valuable medicines.

One may wonder how Columbus, a 41-year-old professional mapmaker, avid reader, researcher and seasoned mariner, a man who had spent the greater part of his adult life planning his great venture to the west, could have been so far off in his calculations. One explanation may be that, as well as a master mariner, he was also a clever politician. As a Christian whose expedition was funded by two Christian monarchs, King Ferdinand II of Aragon and Queen Isabella I of Castile, Columbus's miscalculations may well have been due not to a lack of navigational information--of which there was a great deal available-- but to a calculated decision to use "acceptable" sources of scientific knowledge and to exclude or ignore other, more "foreign" sources.

During the seven centuries of Arab dominion over Spain and Portugal, from AD 711 to 1492, there had developed a culture of Muslim arts and sciences which had a deep and permanent effect on the life, arts and sciences of Europe. The roots of this culture went as far back as Europe's Dark Ages, which can be defined as lasting roughly from AD 476 to 1000, during which the Arab world was the incubator of Western civilization. The Arabs not only preserved, refined, updated and translated into Arabic the rich heritage of classical Greek knowledge, but they also added original and significant new contributions (3)

Once Europe began its explorations of the world of knowledge, it turned not to Greek or Roman sources, most of which were lost or inaccessible, but to Arabic scientific writings. Recognizing this, Europeans in the 12th century embarked on a massive program of translation of these sources, founding a college of translators in Toledo, Spain, from which most of the Arab works on mathematics and astronomy were first made available to Europe's scholars.

During that period and even earlier--in fact, dating back to the days of the Roman Empire (27 BC to AD 284)--people had discussed the idea of sailing west to find the riches of the Golden East. Yet no one had ever tried it.

By the seventh century, however, the Arabs were thoroughly familiar with the eastward approaches to the Orient. For over 300 years they had explored much of the known world. From Delhi and Agra in the east, through Tehran, Baghdad and Damascus, to Cairo, Tripoli, Tunis and Cordoba in the west, Arab scientists and explorers had expanded the knowledge of the known world and pushed back the horizons of the unknown.

Ultimately, this knowledge--along with philosophy, logic, mathematics, natural history and much else--was to be found written down in the great libraries that were the flowers of Spain's brilliant Muslim-Christian-Jewish culture, and in libraries elsewhere in

Europe. Arab geographical encyclopedias, dictionaries, maps and charts, as well as books on mathematics, astronomy and navigation, and treatises on vastly improved navigational instruments, reposed there in Muslim Spain and in the Middle East.

So, too, did the theory of "the new world beyond the Sea of Darkness," the idea of an uncharted continent that lay to the west of the known world. There seems to be little doubt that it was the Arabs who first made the maps that led Columbus to the New World.

Growing up in a major seaport, Columbus could not have escaped hearing about Arab exploits and Arab seafaring skills at an early age. The son of Domenico Colombo, a prosperous weaver, Cristoforo Colombo was born in 1451 and grew up in Genoa. A great cosmopolitan merchant center in the mid-1400's, Genoa had colonies in Egypt, Syria, Cyprus, Constantinople, and on the shores of the Black Sea and the Sea of Azov.

From these far-flung colonies, Genoese merchants, colonists, diplomats and missionaries ventured forth into Anatolia, Georgia, the Caspian Sea, Persia and India. In the mid-15th century, the evantine coast was an open door to the East, ideally situated for trading with the ports of the Black Sea and Asia Minor. Indeed, 200 years earlier, when recording his wondrous tales of his journeys to the Far East, the Venetian traveler Marco Polo wrote of meeting Genoese and Venetian merchants on the Great China Road.

From some of Columbus's letters, we know that he was profoundly affected by Marco Polo's account of his travels.

The prosperous Colombo family lived in a house near the Porta Sant' Andrea, and by his own account, we know that by the time he was 10 years old, the young Columbus loved the bustle of the port. He would linger on the docks and watch the seamen going back and forth from the giant sailing ships crowding the harbor, ships that had arrived across shining seas from far-off and exotic places like Chios and Constantinople, Egypt and Tunis and Syria. He and his friends like to play games among the bales and crates of silk and cotton, the kegs of oil and wine and spices.

Entranced, he would sit down with the sailors, a small blue-eyed, red-haired lad, and listen raptly to their tales of the magical lands to the east. It is hard to imagine that the boy Columbus would not have been stirred by the daring exploits of these sailors, many of them from the Levant--or by the tales he heard later when, as a seagoing lad of 14, sailing out of Genoa, he listened to the shipboard tales of the venturesome Arab traders who roamed the eastern Mediterranean.

He was unlettered and unread in those days. Not until years later did he teach himself to read, and then it was not in his native Italian, but in Castilian Spanish.

By the time Columbus arrived in Portugal, he was somewhere in his mid-20's. The Christians had re-conquered much of Spain and Portugal from the Muslims. Nonetheless, because of the Muslim heritage, the Iberian Peninsula was still Europe's center of intellectual and artistic endeavor. Lisbon, where Columbus lived while planning his voyage into the Atlantic, was the capital of Portugal and a learned city in which it would have been easy for him to get the books and materials he needed to pursue his research. Since his youth, he had learned Spanish, Portuguese, Latin and other languages. It therefore seems likely that Columbus--sailor, navigator, professional cartographer and later son-in-law of one of Henry the Navigator's sea captains--would have drawn on this wealth of Muslim geographical knowledge.

Indeed, Columbus wrote in a letter in 1501 that during his many voyages to all parts of the world, he had met learned men of various races and sects and had "endeavored to see all books of cosmography, history, and philosophy and of other sciences." It is therefore unlikely he would have overlooked the more than four centuries of Muslim science and exploration available to him so close at hand.

According to one of his biographers, the American Samuel Eliot Morison, author of "Admiral of the Ocean Sea", Columbus did some "heavy combing through ancient and medieval authorities on geography" before setting out on his voyage "in order to gather information and ammunition for his next bout with the experts." If this is so, he could hardly have missed such translated works as al-Biruni's "History of India" and Yaqut's "Mu'jam al-Buldan". It would seem also that he would have delved eagerly into Ibn Battuta's 13th-century "Rihlah" (Journey), in which that greatest of early travelers writes about his 120,000-

kilometer (75,000-mile) trip from North Africa to China and back.

2

From several of his other biographers, most notably the Spanish priest Fray Bartolome de las Casas, it is also known that Columbus was an avid reader of books on geography and cosmography. Four of the books he owned have been preserved: a 1485 Latin translation of the "*Book of Ser Marco Polo*", an Italian translation of Pliny's "*Natural History*" printed in 1489, Pierre d'Ailly's "*Imago Mundi*" and minor treatises, and a 1477 edition of the

"Historia   Rerum   Ubique Gestarum" by Pope Pius II.

Columbus also admitted relying heavily on information he gleaned from the school of navigation founded by Prince Henry of Portugal, often known as Henry the Navigator. Around 30 years before Columbus's first voyage, some of the prince's caravels had sailed west, to the outer edge of the Azores and perhaps as far as present-day Newfoundland. Concluding that there were other lands to explore beyond what Ptolemy had described in his second-century *"Guide to Geography"*, and eager to retain and organize the geographical information in the possession of sailors and navigators--many of them from the Levant--the prince established the school at Sagres, in southern Portugal, to act as a sort of clearing house for present and future knowledge of the sea. It may have been from this source that Columbus discovered that when, years earlier, Vasco da Gama had sailed along Africa's east coast, he was guided by an Arab pilot, Ahmad ibn Majid, who used an Arab map then unknown to European sailors.

3

Ibn Majid was one of the personalities this author covered in separate article titles:***Personalities I admire: Arab Navigator: Ahmad ibn Majid, Ras al-Khaimah, UAE.*** (4)

Ahmad ibn Majid was one of the most famous Arab navigators (mu'allim) in history, was born around 1432-1437. at Julfar in northern Ras al-Khaimah, which was part of Oman, until 1970, He became famous in the West as the navigator who has been associated with helping Vasco da Gama find his way from Africa to India, for in a work by the Meccan writer Qutb al-Din al-Nahrawali (1511-1582) entitled al-Barq al-yamani fi'l-fath al-'Uthmani, published in 1892, we read that, having reached East Africa, the Portuguese 'continually sought information regarding [the crossing of] this sea [Arabian Sea] until a skilful sailor named Ahmad ibn Majid put himself at their disposal'.

This is now known to be incorrect. But Ibn Majid's fame in the Arabic speaking world was far greater, for he was the author of nearly 40 works of poetry and prose. The first of these, his Hawiya, is a poem of some 1082 verses dating to 1462 which is a veritable compendium of navigational theory. Ibn Majid's Fawa'id, the full title of which translates as 'the book of profitable things concerning the first principles and rules of navigation', is perhaps the greatest work on Arab navigation ever written. Not only does it provide unrivalled detail on the Indian Ocean, the routes to be used in crossing it, and the region's chief ports, but he provides a history of Arab navigation prior to his time as well.

And yet, despite all this available information, Columbus made a major miscalculation of the distance he had to sail to reach the other side of the globe.

That the earth was a sphere was not a new idea, and it was widely accepted by well-educated people in Columbus's time. So was the Greeks' division of the spherical earth into 360 degrees, but where sources differed was on the question of the length of a degree. The correct measurement, we know today, is about 111kilometers (60 nautical miles) per degree at the equator. In the third century BC, the Libyan-born Greek astronomer Eratosthenes, director of the library at Alexandria, had come up with a remarkably accurate calculation of 100 kilometers (59.5 nautical miles) per degree; in the second century, the great Alexandrian geographer Ptolemy had calculated the degree at 93 kilometers (50 nautical miles). In the ninth century, Muslim astronomer Abu al'Abbas Ahmad al-Farghani, whose works were translated into Latin during the Middle Ages and who--under the name Alfraganus— was studied widely in Europe, had calculated that a degree measured 122 kilometers (about 66 nautical miles)--not as accurate a result as that of Eratosthenes, but better than Ptolemy's.

Either Columbus erroneously used Roman miles in converting al-Farghani's calculations into modern units of distance--thus coming up with a figure of 45 miles per degree at the equator--or, after first deciding that al-Farghani's figure was right, chose in the end, perhaps for reasons of policy, to follow the revered and irrefutable Ptolemy, whose "Geography", in its first printed Latin edition, had gained great popularity in 15th-century Europe. In the first case, Columbus would have underestimated the distance he had to sail to reach Asia by a third; in the second, by some 25 percent.

Had Columbus but accepted the ninth-century findings of a consortium of 70 Muslim scholars, working under the aegis of Caliph 'Abd Allah al-Ma'mun, who had gathered them to determine the length of a degree of latitude, he might have avoided many mistakes.

Using wooden rods as measures, the caliph's scholars traveled a north-south road until they saw a change of one degree in the elevation of the pole star. Their measurements resulted in an amazingly accurate figure for the earth's circumference: 41,526 kilometers, or 22,422 nautical miles--the equivalent of 115.35 kilometers per degree. By Columbus's time, a wealth of knowledge gleaned from Arab science and exploration rested in the libraries of Spain and Portugal. Al-Biruni had accurately determined latitude and longitude and--six hundred years before Galileo—had suggested that the earth rotated on its own axis. One hundred years later, in the ninth century, the mathematician al-Khwarizmi had measured the length of a terrestrial degree and Arab navigators were using magnetic needles to plot accurate courses. It was around this time, too, that the Arab astronomers Ibn Yunus and al-Battani—or Albategnius, as he was known in Europe--improved the ancient astrolabe, the quadrant, the sextant and the compass to the point that, for hundreds of years afterward, no long-distance traveler could venture forth without them. By the 12th century, the Hispano-Arab geographer al-Idrisi had completed his voluminous world atlas containing dozens of maps and charts (5)

In calculating the distances he had to travel to reach India and the Orient, Columbus chose not to rely on the Arab and Muslim sources. He was, instead, greatly persuaded by the theory of Paolo Toscanelli, a

Florentine physician who dabbled in astronomy and mathematics. When he saw Toscanelli's charts stating that Marco Polo's estimate of the length of Asia was correct, and that it was only 3000 miles from Lisbon westward to Japan and 5000 to Hangzhou, China, Columbus accepted the figures he wished most to hear. It was Toscanelli's chart he took with him on his first voyage of discovery. Columbus also believed that his voyage west from Spain to India, though difficult, would be short. Using maps and information based on the calculations of Ptolemy and Martin Behaim, the German cartographer, he believed he could reach China after no more than a 4000-mile voyage. This notion was confirmed by Pierre D''Ailly's "Imago Mundi", a book that, according to Columbus's son and biographer Ferdinand, was his father's bedside companion for years. (Columbus's copy, its margins covered with hundreds of and-written notes, is in the Seville museum.) D'Ailly believed that the western ocean, between Morocco and the eastern coast of Asia, was "of no great width." He followed the system of Marinus of Tyre, a second-century Greek who made Eurasia very wide east to west, and the Atlantic Ocean narrow, and predicted that the latter could be crossed in a few days with a fair wind.

According to Columbus's log--the original of which has been lost, or, as some historians suggest, destroyed--he sailed his tiny fleet of three small ships to the New World by dead reckoning. his means he crossed the vast expanse of Atlantic Ocean between the Canary Islands and the Bahamas using only a mariner's compass and dividers, a quadrant and lead line, an ampolleta, or half-hour glass, a ruler, and charts. His charts were sheepskins that showed the coasts of Spain, Portugal and North Africa, the Azores, Madeira and the Canaries. He took his course from his mariner's compass, developed from the magnetic needle used four centuries before by Arab navigators. His quadrant was an early invention of the great Arab astronomer Ibn Yunus of Cairo.

There is no doubt that Columbus deserves to be celebrated, in this anniversary year, for his courage, perseverance, sailing skills and superb navigational ability. On the other hand, one can only wonder what might have happened that October day 1492 had he heeded eight centuries of Arab invention and navigational knowledge. Certainly it would have made his navigation easier, his fears fewer, and his landfall more accurate.

4

In Conclusion, we may arrive to the finding of this research, which is simply says: Arabs were among those who have the long hand to contribute in Columbus discovery of the New World.

As we wrote in the introduction of this book. "No doubt, the Arabs have a sparkling influence on world thoughts. Arab sciences were on top of world civilization in the age of two great Arab dynasties: the Umayyad and the Abbasid as a continuation product of Islamic thoughts started in the time of

Muhammad and the Guided Caliphs."

These facts cannot be denied taking into consideration that thoughts wordview (Philosophica or Ethical) can be transacted from one culture to another, by many ways diffusion Theorists know very well. In addition, the reports documents found supporting this claim.

Notes:

1. See my book, *Great Arab & Muslim Thinkers*, 2012

2.See "*Aramco World*", November-December 1991.

3. See "*Aramco World*", May-June 1982.

4. Yahya, Hasa. *Personalities I admire: Arab Navigator: Ahmad ibn Majid, Ras al-Khaimah, UAE.* Wordpress Askdryahya Site.(2011)

5. See "*Aramco World*", July-August 1977.

Source:

Aileen Vincent-Barwood, in "Aramco World" (January/February 1992, Vol. 43, No. 1, pp. 5-9)

http://www.millersville.edu/~columbus/data/

Yahya, Hasan. *Columbus Owes Arabs in his Maps in his discovery the the New World* – America - Wordpress Askdryahya site Publication.

Yahya, Hasa. *Personalities I admire: Arab Navigator: Ahmad ibn Majid, Ras al-Khaimah, UAE.* Wordpress Askdryahya Site.(2011)

حول مطبوعات الموسوعة العربية الأمريكية

ومنشورات معهد إحياء التراث العربي في المهاجر

Arab American Encyclopedia-USA - Hasan Yahya

حول الدكتور حسن عبدالقادر يحيى

Dr. Hasan A. Yahya Biographical Skitch

HASAN YAHYA was born at a small village called Majdal-YaFa (Majdal Sadiq) in Mandate Palestine (1944). He migrated as a refugee to Mes-ha, a village east of Kufr Qasim, west of Nablus (in the West Bank), then moved with his family to Zarka, 25 km north of Amman – Jordan. He finished the high school at Zarka Secondary School, 1963. He was appointed as a teacher in the same year. Studied Law first at Damascus University, then Lebanon University. He moved to Kuwait. Where he got married in 1967. He was working at Kuwait Television, taught at bilingual School, and Kuwait University. In 1982, Hasan left to the United States to continue his education at Michigan State University. He got the Master Degree in 1983, the Ph.D degree in 1988 in Education (Psychology of Administration). In 1991, He obtained his post degree in research, the result was a second Ph.D degree in Social Psychology. He was the only Arab student who enrolled ever to pursue two simultaneous Ph.D programs from Michigan State University .

Professor Yahya employment history began as a supervisor of a joint project to rehabilitate Youth (inmates out of prison) by Michigan State University and Intermediate School Districts. Worked also as a Teacher Assistant and lecturer in the same university. He was offered a position at Lansing Community College as well as Jackson Community College where he was assistant professor, then associate professor, then full professor (1991-2006). He taught Sociology, psychology, education, criminology and research methods. He supervised 19 Master and Ph.D candidates on various personal, economic psychological and social development topics. Professor Yahya published Hundreds of articles and research reports in local, regional, and international journals. His interest covers local, regional and global conflicts. He also authored, translated, edited and published over 200 books in several languages, in almost all fields especial education, sociology and psychology. He also, was a visiting professor at Easterm Michigan University to give Conflict Management courses. Prof. Yahya accepted an offer to join Zayed University Faculty Team in 1998, then he served as the Head of Education and Psychology Department at Ajman University of Science and Technology 2001-04.

Dr. Yahya established several institutes in Diaspora, the Arab American Encyclopedia, Ihyaa al Turath al Arabi Project, (Revival of Arab Heritage in Diaspora.Recently he was nominated for honorary committee member for the Union of Arab and Muslim Writers in America, and accepted to be a board member in International Journal of Humanities Studies. He was affiliated with sociological associations and was a member of the Association of Muslim Social Scientists (AMSS) at USA. Social Activities and Community Participation: Dr. Yahya was a national figure on Diversity and Islamic Issues in the United States, with special attention to Race Relations and Psychology of Assimilation. He was invited as a public speaker to many TV shows and interviews in many countries. His philosophy includes enhancing knowledge to appreciate the others, and to compromise with others in order to live peacefully with others. This philosophy was the backgrounds of his theory, called " Theory C. of Conflict Management". And developed later to a Science of Cultural Normalization under the title: "Crescentology. The results of such theory will lead to world peace depends on a global Knowledge, Understanding, appreciation, and Compromising (KUAC)" (Revised Feb. 2013)

ولد الدكتور حسن عبدالقادر يحيى في مجدل يابا من أعمال يافا – فلسطين عام 1944. تلقى علومه الابتدائية في مدرسة بديا الأميرية في الضفة الغربية أيام احتوائها ضمن المملكة الأردنية الهاشمية وتخرج في جامعة بيروت حاملاً الإجازة في اللغة العربية وآدابها، ودبلوم التأهيل التربوي من كلية القديس يوسف بلبنان، ودبلوم الدراسات العليا (الماجستير) ودكتوراة في الإدارة التربوية من جامعة ولاية ميشيغان بالولايات المتحدة عام 1988، وشهادة الدكتوراه في علم الاجتماع المقارن من الجامعة نفسها عام 1991. عمل في التدريس والصحافة الأدبية. أديب وشاعر

وقاص ، منصرف إلى الكتابة في علوم كثيرة تخص علمي النفس والاجتماع والتنمية البشرية ، ألف ونشر العديد من المقالات (1000 +) والكتب باللغتين العربية والإنجليزية (أكثر من 200 كتابا) ، منها ست مجموعات قصصية وست كتب للأطفال ، وأربع دواوين شعرية باللغتين أيضا. وعدد من كتب التراث في الشعر والأدب والأخلاق الإسلامية والتربية والأديان . وهو الآن أستاذ متقاعد في جامعة ولاية ميشيغان. . وكان عضوا سابقا في جمعية العلماء المسلمين في أمريكا . وهو مؤسس الموسوعة العربية الأمريكية في الولايات المتحدة ضمن مشروع إحياء التراث العربي في بلاد المهجرز كما تم ترشيحه مؤخرا ليكون عضو مجلس التحرير لمجلة الدراسات الإنسانية العالمية.

Arab American Encyclopedia Publications

منشورات الموسوعة العربية الأمريكية

Dr. Hasan Yahya Books - كتب الدكتور: د حسن يحيى

كتب (بالعربية والإنجليزية) ، قام بنشرها الدكتور حسن يحيى ضمن مشروعه: إحياء التراث العربي في المهجر ، بالتعاون مع الموسوعة العربية الأمريكية التي أسسها أيضا لهذا الغرض ومعهد البحوث الإدارية ومطابع شركة القدس والبركان وتلفزيون الدكتور يحيى في الولايات المتحدة .

The Arab American Encyclopedia (Hasan Yahya) Publications:

In English:

1. Hammurabi Codes of Law
2. *The Dangers of the GMS and Conflict Management: Research Paper, Slideshow & Presentation*
3. Moon Flowers: Poems, Tales & Politics
4. Poetry Diwan: Love, Fears & Hopes
5. Crescentology: A Theory Of Conflict Management And Cultural Normalization
6. Crescentologism: The Moon Theory
7. Brief Arab & Muslim Ethics: For Non-Arabic Speakers (Bilingual)
8. The Beast In Me America: Arabic Folklore, Tales, Stories, & Poetry
9. Personality & Stress Management: A New Theory
10. Arab Palestinian & Jews: Sociological Aproach
11. Legal Adultery: Sexuality & World Cultures
12. Crescentologism: The Moon Theory
13. Islam: Finds Its Way

14. 30 Tales From Faraway Land: Middle Eastern
15. Brief Islamic History (bilingual)
16. Jesus Christ Speaks Arabic
17. Fan Adabi Jadid (bilingual)
18. Protocols of Zion: Trilingual : Spnaish, English & Arabic
19. Prophets Saga: from Adam to Muhammad
20. Al-Akhlaq al-Islamiyyah (Bilingual)
21. Quotes: Love & Humor (Bilingual)
22. Jesus is Different the Prophets History
23. 50 Short Stories (55 words)-Bilingual
24. The Intruder: Bilingual
25. *Alisha and Other Stories.*
26. 70 Very Short Stories (English)
27. *Short Stories from World Literature (Bilingual)*
28. 65 stories for Children 3-12 , (English)
29. Occupation and Other Stories from World Literature –English
30. 85 Fables & Tales for Children 3 to 12 (English)
31. *Naji al-Ali Art Show.* A Palestinian Artist *Ann Mary Thatcher*
32. Princess Imagination: A New Design Novel (English)
33. Al-Hariri Assemblies (Maqamat al-Hariri (English)
34. Water, Population and Conflict in the Middle East.
35. *Princess Diana Still Alive, A New Novel Design. Ann Mary Thatcher.*
36. *Nietzsche On Christianity*
37. *Bertrand Russell: Roads to Freedom*
38. *Ernest HemingwaySuicide Story*
39. *Brief Management: Theories & Applications.*
40. *I Have the Right to be Angry*
41. *FBI Madness Storm , One Act Play*
42. *Nadia: An Innocent Girl from Cairo, Short Story*
43. *Brain and Mind Psychology*
44. *Banning Islam: Petition of Ignorance*
45. *The Wiseman Spirit Still Dancing:Short Story*
46. *The Oldman and the Mower, Short Story*
47. *Al Imam al Bukhari Research Methods*
48. *Secularism: A Response to Sh. Yusuf al Qaradawi*
49. *Family, Leadership & Problem Solving Games*
50. *Knowledge & Globalization*
51. *Islam & Muslims in America: Sociological Analysis*
52. *The Science of Socio-Therapy*
53. *Defending Islam, Banning Islam*
54. *Defeating PTSD Epidemics*